Who Was Alexander Graham Bell?

by Bonnie Bader

illustrated by David Groff

Penguin Workshop

To Lauren and Allie—may you, like Bell, follow your own
interests and see where they take you—BB

PENGUIN WORKSHOP
An Imprint of Penguin Random House LLC, New York

Text copyright © 2013 by Bonnie Bader.
Illustrations copyright © 2013 by David Groff.
Cover illustration copyright © 2013 by Penguin Random House LLC. All rights reserved.
Published by Penguin Workshop, an imprint of Penguin Random House LLC, New York.
PENGUIN and PENGUIN WORKSHOP are trademarks of Penguin Books Ltd.
WHO HQ & Design is a registered trademark of Penguin Random House LLC.
Printed in the USA.

Visit us online at www.penguinrandomhouse.com.

Library of Congress Control Number: 2013024903

ISBN 9780448464602

20 19 18 17

Contents

Who Was
Alexander Graham Bell?

One day in 1858, two young boys named
Aleck and Ben were horsing around in a flour

mill owned by Ben's father. The boys leaped over
bags of flour and ran past machines that ground
up wheat. They were having fun. But they were
bothering the mill workers who needed to do their
work. Finally, Ben's father called the boys into his
office. He told them to find something useful to
do. What exactly would that be? Aleck wanted to

know. Ben's father picked up a handful of grain. Each piece of grain was covered in a thick husk. It would be useful if they could figure out a good way to get the husks off the wheat grain.

The boys accepted the challenge. First, they scraped the husks off with a nailbrush. It

worked, but it took too long. They needed a faster way. Aleck thought about the problem some more. He was good at solving problems. He remembered seeing a large vat with spinning paddles at the mill. The boys went and watched the vat at work. At last, Aleck had an idea. What if stiff brushes, like big nailbrushes, were attached to the vat's paddles? When the paddle-brushes began spinning, the husks would be scraped off the wheat—fast!

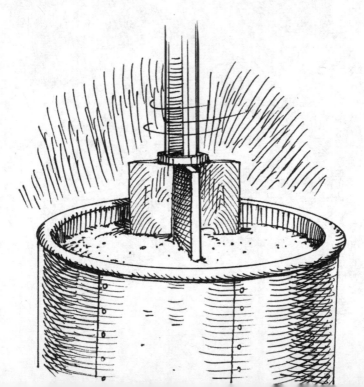

Aleck presented his idea to Ben's father. The mill owner liked what he heard and put it to the test. Aleck's idea worked! Maybe it's not so surprising that this eleven-year-old boy grew up to become a world-famous inventor—the man who invented the telephone.

Chapter 1
An Inventor Is Born

On March 3, 1847, in Edinburgh, Scotland, a baby boy was born into the Bell family. He was named Alexander after both his grandfather and his father.

Grandfather Bell lived in London and was a teacher. He helped young people with speech problems, such as stuttering. Grandfather Bell studied the way spoken words are formed. He learned how important the lungs and vocal cords are for speaking. He studied the way the lips and the face moved, too.

Alexander's father, called Melville, taught speech, too. From the moment baby Alexander was born, it was expected that he would follow in the other Alexanders' footsteps.

But what interested little Aleck, as his family called him, was exploring. This boy, with a pale face, brown eyes, and dark bushy hair, loved roaming the Scottish countryside with his brothers, Melly and Ted. Aleck collected all kinds of plants, rocks, and animal skeletons.

Onc summer day in 1850, the Bell family went on a picnic. Young Aleck wandered off to explore. A nearby wheat field caught his eye. He walked into the tall wheat and sat down. Closing his eyes, he wondered if

he could hear the wheat growing. He strained his ears and listened. But he heard nothing.

After a while, Aleck decided to return to the picnic. But he couldn't find his way out of the wheat field. The wheat was too high. Aleck was lost! He yelled for help. No one heard him. Little Aleck sat on the ground and cried until he fell asleep. Later, he awoke to his father calling his name. Aleck was safe! Sometimes curiosity could get a boy in trouble!

Although Aleck was smart, he was not a good student. Greek, Latin, math, and science—they all bored him. Plants and animals were much more interesting. He also loved music. And he learned to become an excellent pianist from his mother, Eliza.

It was amazing that Mrs. Bell could play the piano so well. Why? Because she was nearly deaf. She needed an ear tube to help her hear. To play the piano, she put one end of the tube in her ear, and the other against the piano. That way, she could feel, or hear, the beautiful sounds of the music.

Aleck was very close to his mother. Although most people shouted into her ear tube, Aleck liked to put his mouth on her forehead and speak softly.

And this worked! Eliza Bell was able to hear what her son said. How was that possible? Eliza picked up the vibrations that Aleck's words made when he put his lips on her head. A vibration is a steady movement or quiver. By talking to his mother this way, Aleck began to understand how sounds travel and are heard.

Eliza Bell encouraged Aleck to be curious and creative. But his father did not always approve. He wanted his middle son to be a good student like his brothers. Melville Bell often interrupted Aleck's piano lessons. He'd drag the boy into the living room where Melville discussed science with friends. For Aleck, it was boring, boring, boring.

Even as a young boy, Aleck wanted to be his own person. In fact, he was so independent that he chose a middle name for himself. It was just before he turned eleven. A family friend named Alexander Graham came to visit. Aleck liked the sound of the man's name. From that day on, Aleck decided he would be called Alexander Graham Bell.

Chapter 2
A Turning Point

In 1862, Aleck finished high school. His father was still concerned about his middle son's lack of focus. The answer, Melville decided, was to send Aleck to London to live with Grandfather Bell. Aleck did not want to leave his mother or brothers. But Aleck was put on the train anyway. Aleck didn't know it, but he was setting off on a journey that would change his life.

SCOTLAND

Edinburgh

North Sea

ENGLAND

London

London was a very busy place. At the time, it was the world's largest city. There were palaces, grand cathedrals, many theaters, and the Houses of Parliament, where the people in the government met. Aleck was not used to seeing so many people in one place. Edinburgh was smaller. The air was cleaner. London was filled with pollution. The two cities were as different as could be.

Aleck also found living with Grandfather Bell very different. There were so many rules! One rule was that he had to dress like a gentleman. Whenever Aleck stepped outside, he had to wear a dark suit, a stiff white shirt, and a tie. But that was not all. He also had to wear a top hat and gloves, and carry a cane!

Another rule was that Aleck had to study—
six days a week! Many of the subjects, like Latin
and history, still bored Aleck. But it was thrilling
to sit and watch his grandfather give speech
lessons to students.

Grandfather Bell let Aleck travel around London by himself. Often, Aleck went to the library. There, he read many books on sound. Later, Aleck wrote, "This period of my life seems the turning point of my whole career." Indeed, it changed him from a carefree boy into a more serious young man, eager to learn.

SIR CHARLES
WHEATSTONE

When the year was up, Melville came to London. Before bringing his son home, they visited a famous inventor named Sir Charles Wheatstone. Sir Charles showed the Bells an invention of his. It was a wooden box that had an accordion-like bag on one side. The bag was called a bellows. On the other side there were levers and a leather tube. The tube led to a reed. (A reed is used in musical instruments such as the saxophone). Sir Charles squeezed the bellows, pushing out air. At the same time, he squeezed the leather tube and moved the levers. The moving air made the reed vibrate, and out came words! The words were hard to understand, but still—the machine talked!

Back in Edinburgh, Melville challenged Aleck

and Melly to create a speaking box like Charles Wheatstone's. Only theirs had to be better.

The brothers got to work. Melly made the "lungs" and the "throat." Aleck made the "tongue" and the "mouth." It was important to shape the tongue, lips, and mouth carefully. If not, words would not come out clearly.

After putting their speaking machine together, they took it to the bottom of the stairway in their

house. Melly blew through the throat, which he had made out of tin. Aleck worked the parts of the mouth. Finally sounds came out. "Mamma, mamma," a little voice said. The voice sounded so real, the Bells' upstairs neighbors thought a baby was crying.

Melly and Aleck had met their father's challenge. Indeed, the talking machine started Aleck on the path that led to his invention of the telephone.

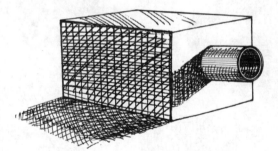

Chapter 3
An Ear for Sound

At sixteen, Aleck felt too old to still be living at home. He thought about packing his bags and running away to become a sailor. But then an ad in a newspaper caught his eye. The Weston House Academy in Elgin, Scotland, needed a teacher. Actually, the school needed *two* teachers—a music teacher and a speech teacher. Without telling their father, Aleck and Melly both applied to the school. But the brothers made one big mistake. They listed their father as a reference on their applications! (A reference is a person who will say how wonderful a job you'd do.)

A letter came from Weston House Academy to Melville asking for a reference. At first, Melville was furious. How dare his sons go behind his

back! But in time, Melville realized that sending his sons away was not such a bad idea. So Melly was sent to the University of Edinburgh for a year. Aleck was sent to Weston House Academy to study and teach.

Alexander Graham Bell spent the 1863 school year at Weston. Although younger than some of his students, Aleck proved to be an excellent

WESTON HOUSE ACADEMY

teacher. And by the time he returned home that summer, he discovered that his father had invented a new and wonderful way to help teach deaf people to speak. It was called Visible Speech.

Melville and his sons traveled through Scotland to show how Visible Speech worked. During demonstrations, Melville would ask one of his sons to leave the room. Then an audience member would say something—a sound, a word, or even a word in another language. Melville would write it down on a blackboard, using Visible Speech symbols. The boy would come back into the room, read the symbols, and make the sound

or word. Aleck or Melly got it right every time!
Once, Aleck read the symbols and heard himself
making a strange noise. The crowd clapped wildly.
Aleck had correctly read and copied the sound for
sawing wood.

The trip got Aleck more and more interested in speech. Take vowel sounds, for instance. Some vowel sounds were higher in pitch than others. *Pitch* is a musical term that tells how high or low a sound is. A higher pitch has a higher number of vibrations. Aleck would stand in front of a mirror and pronounce vowel sounds. He saw that the shape of his mouth and throat created the different pitches of these vowel sounds. For example, when he said an *e* it had a higher pitch than when he said an *o*. And his mouth and throat moved differently, too.

VISIBLE SPEECH

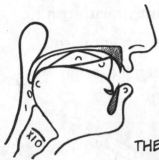

ALEXANDER MELVILLE BELL DEVELOPED THE VISIBLE SPEECH SYSTEM IN 1864. IT WAS A WAY FOR DEAF PEOPLE TO READ SOUNDS AND THEN MAKE THOSE SOUNDS THEMSELVES. THE VISIBLE SPEECH METHOD BROKE DOWN WORDS INTO SIMPLE SOUNDS, AND USED A SYMBOL FOR EACH SOUND. THE SYMBOLS SHOWED EXACTLY HOW TO SHAPE THE TONGUE, LIPS, THROAT, AND MOUTH FOR THE SOUND. BY READING THE SYMBOLS, A DEAF PERSON COULD COPY THE SOUNDS AND SPEAK WORDS. MELVILLE WANTED VISIBLE SPEECH TO BE THE ONLY WAY DEAF PEOPLE LEARNED TO COMMUNICATE. LATER ON, HOWEVER, SIGN LANGUAGE BECAME THE PREFERRED WAY FOR DEAF STUDENTS TO COMMUNICATE.

Aleck began thinking about the sounds of words and musical tones. Were they the same in some ways? He started to experiment with tuning forks. A tuning fork is metal instrument with two prongs shaped like a *U*. When a tuning fork is hit, it "sings out" a specific pitch. This is why tuning forks are used to tune musical instruments. The sound that a tuning fork makes sends sound waves into the air. Whenever Aleck hit a tuning fork to make it vibrate, he'd sing the pitch that the tuning fork made. Aleck put the vibrating tuning fork next to his mouth while he silently mouthed vowel sounds. When one of his vowel sounds made the tuning fork vibrate faster, he knew he had found the vowel's pitch. He was right—speech and musical tones were alike!

It turned out that a scientist in Germany had noticed the same thing. Aleck read about his experiments. The trouble was that the information was in German. Aleck knew some German, but not much. He thought the scientist had sent vowel sounds electrically over telegraph wires.

The German scientist had *not* done that. But the idea of sending voice sounds over telegraph wires got Aleck's mind going. Think of it! A talking telegraph! It would change the way people got in touch with each other. Was it possible to actually invent such a machine?

THE TELEGRAPH

THE WORD *TELEGRAPH* MEANS TO "WRITE FAR." WHEN SOMEONE SENDS A TELEGRAM, THE MESSAGE QUICKLY REACHES SOMEONE FAR AWAY. SAMUEL MORSE INVENTED THE TELEGRAPH IN 1835. TO SEND A MESSAGE, AN OPERATOR PRESSED DOWN ON A METAL LEVER ON A TELEGRAPH MACHINE TO SEND, OR MAKE, A SERIES OF ELECTRICAL CURRENTS. THE CURRENTS THEN TRAVELED ACROSS ELECTRICAL WIRES TO ANOTHER TELEGRAPH MACHINE. EACH TIME THE OPERATOR RELEASED THE LEVER, THE ELECTRICAL CURRENT BROKE. DOTS AND DASHES, KNOWN AS MORSE CODE, WERE ASSIGNED TO THE AMOUNTS OF TIME THAT THE CONNECTION LASTED. THESE COULD THEN BE TRANSLATED INTO MESSAGES.

Chapter 4
Endings and Beginnings

On April 23, 1865, Grandfather Bell died. It was a sad time for the Bells and also a turning point for the family. Melville decided to move his family to London, where he planned to take over his father's business. But tragedy soon struck again. Eighteen-year-old Ted Bell fell sick. And in May 1867, he died from a lung disease called tuberculosis. Three years after that, Aleck's older brother and good friend, Melly, died from the same disease.

TED BELL

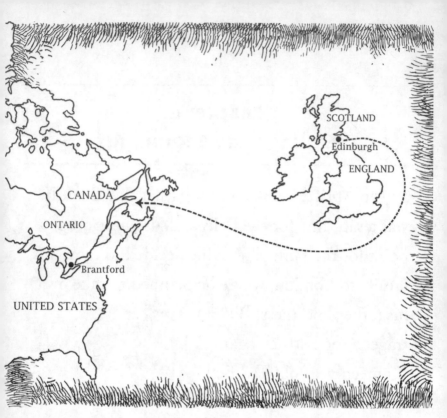

The Bells were heartbroken. Eliza and Melville were frightened. What if their remaining son caught the deadly disease, too? Aleck did not look well lately. He complained of headaches. Eliza decided a change was needed, a big change.

Eliza, Melville, and Aleck moved across the Atlantic to Canada! They lived in a big farmhouse in Brantford, Ontario. The air was crisp. It was beautiful country. Aleck rested and grew well again. Of course he didn't just rest—he spent time experimenting with sound. Soon he felt it was time to get on with his life. So in April 1871, Aleck moved to Boston, Massachusetts. He landed a job teaching at the well-known Boston School for the Deaf.

Aleck was a very good teacher. Patient, too. Using his father's Visible Speech system, many of his students, who hadn't uttered a sound before, started to speak! Their parents were amazed. Word spread. More and more parents sent their children to the school.

Aleck also gave private lessons. One of his students was only five years old. His name was George Sanders. He was the son of a rich

businessman named Thomas Sanders. George
was born deaf. He had never spoken a word. He
couldn't communicate.

Aleck taught George to read and spell by
making a special glove with the alphabet on it.

Soon George could spell the names of his toys. And before long, he could ask for anything he wanted, just by spelling out the words. George's father was very pleased.

Aleck was always looking for the next new way to help people speak and communicate. By 1872, the Western Union Telegraph Company was able to send two messages over the same telegraph wires at the same time. *Two* messages? Aleck was amazed! Up until now, only one message could be sent at a time. Aleck started thinking. If it was possible to send two messages at a time, why couldn't many messages be sent? Maybe there was a way to send the vibration of a tuning fork down a telegraph wire to make a tuning fork at the other end vibrate at the exact same pitch. And if several pairs of tuning forks were used, perhaps Aleck could even send many sounds at once. Aleck called this idea a harmonic, or multiple, telegraph. Now he just had to find a way to create it!

Aleck was lucky. He was offered a job at
Boston University. It was an honor for a man
who had no college degree himself. Aleck earned
a good salary; he also kept working with private
students, like George. And he had a new place to
live—two rooms in a big house that belonged to

George's grandmother. Aleck used one room just for his experiments. Alexander Graham Bell was only twenty-six years old, and boy, did his future look bright!

Chapter 5
A New Direction

Alexander Graham Bell was one busy guy. During the summer of 1874, he went to Brantford to rest. Well, he really didn't rest that much! Now Aleck wanted to fool around with a machine called the phonautograph.

When a sound was made, a pen drew a wavy pattern on a plate of glass. This showed the waves that a sound made.

Aleck began thinking really hard. If sound waves could make a pen move, then maybe they could move other things, too—like a device that could produce an electric current. Perhaps spoken words could be sent across a telegraph wire. Then someone else far away could hear the words! Aha! Although he didn't know it at the time, Aleck was having a brainstorm. This giant idea would lead him much closer to creating the first telephone.

Did Aleck *only* think about inventions? No. He was also very interested in a young sixteen-year-old woman from Boston named Mabel Hubbard. She had been deaf since childhood and was one of Aleck's students. Mabel could lip-read, but her speech was not clear. Mabel's parents, Gertrude and Gardiner Greene Hubbard, hoped Aleck could help her.

Although Mabel thought Aleck was a good teacher, she did not like him when they first met. His face was pale, and he had a big nose and a bushy black mustache and beard. She thought he dressed badly. (She also thought Aleck was much older than he really was.) And she did not think he was a gentleman. Still, Mabel's father,

Gardiner Greene Hubbard, liked Aleck. And more importantly, he hoped Aleck could invent a new kind of telegraph.

Gardiner Hubbard did not approve of the Western Union Telegraph Company. It was the only company that sent telegraphs. Nobody else was able to compete with it. That meant Western Union could charge customers a lot of money to send a telegram. However, if someone else invented another kind of telegraph, then customers would have a choice of which company to use. Prices on telegrams would have to drop. Maybe that someone could be Alexander Graham Bell. Mr. Hubbard offered money to Aleck to continue his work. Many other men, such as the inventor Elisha Gray, were trying to invent their own kind of multiple telegraphs. Mr. Hubbard wanted Aleck to be the first.

ELISHA GRAY

ELISHA GRAY WAS BORN ON A FARM IN BARNESVILLE, OHIO, ON AUGUST 2, 1835. HE HAD MANY JOBS OVER THE YEARS—INCLUDING BLACKSMITH, BOAT BUILDER, AND CARPENTER. BUT WHAT INTERESTED HIM MOST WAS EXPERIMENTING WITH ELECTRICITY. LIKE BELL, GRAY THOUGHT IT WAS POSSIBLE TO TRANSMIT MULTIPLE MESSAGES ACROSS A TELEGRAPH WIRE. GRAY BECAME A BIG RIVAL OF BELL, AS BOTH MEN RACED TO BECOME THE FIRST TO INVENT BOTH THE HARMONIC TELEGRAPH AND THE TELEPHONE.

Chapter 6
A Sound Is Heard

Alexander Graham Bell should have been happy. George Sanders's father, Thomas, had also agreed to give Bell money to work on a new telegraph. The three men signed an agreement. A partnership was formed. But Aleck wasn't satisfied. Figuring out how to send multiple messages across telegraph wires didn't really stir his curiosity. What he wanted to do was send his own *voice* across a wire. But how? He needed help. And he knew just where to get it.

One day, in 1874, Aleck stormed into the Charles Williams Electrical Supply Company in Boston, where he often went to buy supplies for projects he was working on. But today, Aleck wasn't interested in buying anything. He wanted to talk to someone in the shop. Aleck found twenty-year-old Thomas Watson busy at work. Thomas was sharp and smart. He was a skilled craftsman who could take an idea for an invention and build it.

Right away, Aleck began quizzing Thomas about different equipment. Quickly Aleck determined that Thomas was just the man

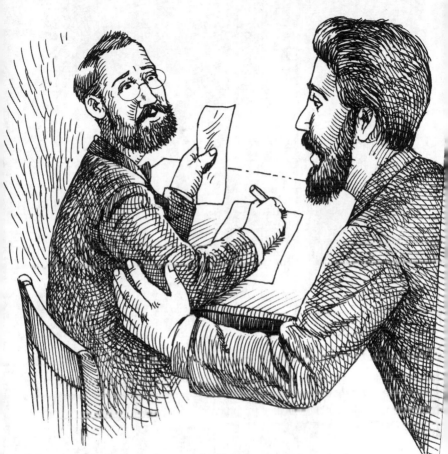

he needed to help make his new telegraph
machine—and maybe even figure out how to
make a telephone. That very day, Thomas Watson
became Alexander Graham Bell's important
assistant.

The two men did not give up their day jobs. Aleck continued teaching and Thomas stayed at the supply shop. Then at night, they worked together in the shop's attic. Aleck owed it to Mr. Hubbard and Mr. Sanders to keep working on the harmonic telegraph. So he and Thomas struggled with that problem while Aleck also shared his dream of inventing a telephone.

Thomas was excited. But unfortunately, Mr. Hubbard and Mr. Sanders weren't. Who would want to hear someone's voice over the wires? Who would buy such a device? No,

THOMAS WATSON

THOMAS WATSON WAS BORN IN SALEM, MASSACHUSETTS, IN 1854. HIS FATHER OWNED A STABLE WHERE HE RENTED OUT HORSES AND CARRIAGES. THOMAS WASN'T INTERESTED IN FOLLOWING IN HIS FATHER'S FOOTSTEPS. BORED WITH SCHOOL, THOMAS GOT HIS FIRST JOB AS A BOOKKEEPER AT THE AGE OF SIXTEEN. BUT THAT BORED HIM, TOO. SO HE WORKED AS A CARPENTER. THAT WASN'T EXCITING, EITHER. WHEN HE LANDED A JOB AT CHARLES WILLIAMS'S MACHINE SHOP IN BOSTON, HE KNEW HE HAD FOUND HIS PASSION. IT WAS THERE THAT HE MET ALEXANDER GRAHAM BELL. THE INVENTION OF THE TELEPHONE MADE WATSON A RICH MAN. HE LATER STARTED THE LARGEST SHIPBUILDING BUSINESS IN AMERICA, AND THEN TURNED TO ACTING AND PLAYWRITING. THOMAS WATSON DIED IN 1934.

a new kind of telegraph was the way to go. They told Aleck to work on that—and just that. If he refused to listen to them, they would not give him any more money.

Aleck did not want to fight with Mr. Hubbard or Mr. Sanders. Especially Mr. Hubbard. Was it because he was afraid of the man? No. Aleck was now deeply in love with Mabel Hubbard. Aleck was twenty-eight years old. Mabel was just seventeen. Her parents told Aleck that he would have to wait a year before taking her on dates.

It was now June 1875. Aleck was frustrated. He and Thomas had been trying to use tuning forks to send sounds down electrical wires. But that was a mistake. Aleck saw that now. Thomas suggested trying reeds to send messages instead. When the reeds vibrated, they made sounds.

The two men went into separate rooms to try sending each other messages. Thomas went into one room with the "transmitter." The transmitter would send the sounds. Aleck went into the room with the "receiver." The receiver would hear the sounds. A long wire connected them. Thomas tried to make the reeds vibrate to produce sound. But one was stuck. So, he plucked at the reed until it became unstuck.

A ping rang out in the receiver that Aleck was holding. "Watson, what did you do?" Aleck called 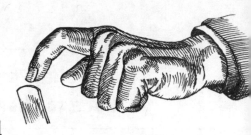 out excitedly. He had heard the sound from way down the hall. Plucking the reed had created a current that was able to travel across the wire into Aleck's room! It was an "Aha!" moment. Aleck was right after all—sound *could* travel across wires. And if the "pinging" sound could travel, then so could the sound of a human voice. Thomas later wrote, "The speaking telephone was born at that moment."

Chapter 7
Race to the Finish

Naturally, Aleck was excited about this discovery. He started making sketches of what the telephone might look like. But he also felt guilty because he was spending so much time working on the telephone. So Aleck wrote Mr. Hubbard a letter to explain what had been occupying his

Dear Mr. Hubbard
I have accidently made a
discovery of the very
greatest importance.

A. Graham Bell

time. "Dear Mr. Hubbard, I have accidentally
made a discovery of the very greatest importance,"
he began.

Mr. Hubbard, however, was still not impressed.
He even hinted that if Aleck didn't give up
the telephone, he could forget about becoming
Mabel's boyfriend!

Aleck wrote Hubbard another letter. In it he
said, "If she [Mabel] does not come to love me
well enough to accept me whatever my profession
or business may be—I do not want her at all."

Luckily, Aleck didn't need to worry about
Mabel's feelings for him. She had come to love
Aleck very deeply. On her eighteenth birthday—
November 25, 1875—she agreed to marry him.

Mabel, however, had one request. She wanted Aleck to drop the "k" in his nickname, because she thought *Alec* sounded more American. That was okay with Alexander Graham Bell, who from then on was known as Alec. The two married on July 11, 1877.

Mabel was always telling Alec not to work so hard. But Alec couldn't change. The telephone was always on his mind now. Step by step, Alec and Thomas were making progress on a model for it. Here's how it worked: Alec spoke into a mouthpiece with a tight covering (it looked like the top of a drum). The sound waves from his voice made the covering vibrate. Those vibrations set in motion an electrical current that reproduced and carried voice sounds. The problem  was the sounds were hard to understand. Alec knew he was close, but he was not there yet.

By this time, Mr. Hubbard and Mr. Sanders saw that Alec was on to something. They urged Alec to get a patent for his model before anyone else did. A patent from the US government is proof that a particular inventor came up with the idea for an invention first and that the idea belongs to him or her. Alec preferred to wait until his telephone worked a lot better. But Alec's partners were too nervous.

On February 14, 1876, without telling Alec, Mr. Hubbard and Mr. Sanders filed the paperwork with the government. The patent for the telephone was theirs. And it was a lucky thing

that they had rushed to file. Just two hours later, Elisha Gray tried to claim the same patent. Gray thought his model for the telephone was better, and more advanced, than Bell's. But now that didn't matter. Elisha Gray was too late. He lost the race to invent the telephone. Alexander Graham Bell had won!

Chapter 8
Famous Words

On March 7, 1876, US patent number 174,465 was awarded to Bell for his telephone. Now, all he and Thomas had to do was create one that really worked!

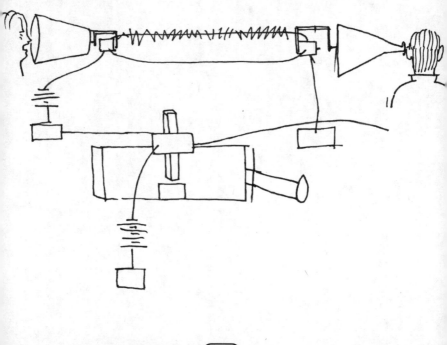

And only three days later, they did. As usual, Bell and Thomas were working in their lab. According to Thomas, Alec was in one room holding a mouthpiece. Thomas was in another room with a receiver pressed against his ear. All of a sudden, over the receiver, Thomas heard Alec say, "Watson—come here—I want to see you!" It sounded as if Alec was in trouble. Alarmed, Thomas ran to Alec. But Alec wasn't hurt. In fact, he looked incredibly happy. Why? Because Alec

realized that Thomas had heard and understood Alec's words over the telephone wire!

Later, Alec wrote to his father, saying, "This is a great day with me. I feel that I have at last struck the solution of a great problem—and the day is coming when [telephone] wires will be laid onto houses just like water or gas—and friends converse with each other without leaving home."

1876 was not only a great year for Alexander Graham Bell. It was also an important year for the United States. The country was turning one hundred. To celebrate, there was a gigantic fair in Philadelphia. It was called the Centennial Exposition.

Almost ten million people came to see exhibits
of art, food, new gadgets, and more. Mr. Hubbard
wanted Alec to show off his telephone at the fair.
Perhaps he would win a prize. But Alec did not
want to go. He was too busy at work in Boston.
He had classes to teach, and he did not want to
leave Mabel behind. Plus, Elisha Gray, who by now

had a patent for the multiple telegraph, would be showing off his invention in Western Union's big fancy exhibit. Bell was sure that people would be more interested in seeing Gray's invention at work.

In the end, Mabel convinced Alec to attend the fair. He set up his telephone in a small corner of the large convention hall. The hall was hot and stuffy. Alec was growing impatient. Not many people had come to see his invention. Nor had any of the judges stopped at his booth yet. Then one of the judges, Don Pedro II—the emperor of Brazil—spotted Alec. He had once visited Alec at the Boston School for the Deaf and remembered him.

Perhaps Alec had something interesting to show.

The emperor crossed the floor to Alec's exhibit stand, and the other judges followed. One of them picked up the receiver of Alec's telephone and put it to his ear. Alec went to the other side of the hall and spoke into the mouthpiece. The judge was astonished—he had heard Alec clearly!

Now it was the emperor's turn. Excitedly, he picked up the receiver. A moment later, he jumped out of his chair and yelled, "I have heard! I have heard!"

Alec received the Gold Medal for Electrical Equipment.

Even more important, word of the telephone started to spread. Alec knew there was still much more to do. The telephone had only been tested across short distances. That wasn't good enough. So Alec did what he always did. He got back to work!

Chapter 9
Victory!

Alec and Thomas began giving lectures and demonstrations of the new incredible device. Over time, Alec made improvements to his invention.

At first, he and Thomas had to be in the same hall to show the phone in action. Soon, though, one of them could be two miles away, then eight, then twenty, and then thirty-two. These were considered long-distance calls!

Newspapers ran articles about the telephone. People were certainly curious. Yet, not many people wanted to buy one. This was terrible news after all of Alec's work and all of Mr. Hubbard's and Mr. Sanders's money.

Mr. Hubbard had an idea. Why not sell the Western Union Company the rights to the telephone? Mr. Hubbard went to see the head of Western Union and asked for $100,000. Then Western Union could sell Alec's telephone. But the answer was no! Western Union said that they already had other inventors working on new and better telephones. Inventors like Thomas Edison and Elisha Gray.

Elisha Gray. That man really worried Bell. There were stories claiming that Gray had really invented the telephone. Alec was hurt. He wrote Gray a letter. Gray apologized and said publicly that credit for inventing the telephone did not belong to him.

Alec's telephone belonged to him. And fortunately, things started to look up. Telephone orders began coming in. People understood how this device would change their lives. On July 9, 1877, Alexander Graham Bell, Thomas Watson, Gardiner Greene Hubbard, and George Sanders formed the Bell Telephone Company. The new company would make telephones and earn lots of money—the men were sure of it!

THOMAS EDISON

THOMAS ALVA EDISON WAS BORN ON
FEBRUARY 11, 1847. AS A BOY, HE DID POORLY IN
SCHOOL, BUT HE GREW UP TO BECOME ONE OF
THE MOST FAMOUS—AND IMPORTANT—INVENTORS
OF ALL TIME. AMONG THE THINGS HE INVENTED
WERE THE PHONOGRAPH AND THE LONG-LASTING
LIGHTBULB. HE ALSO IMPROVED THE TELEGRAPH,
ENABLING IT TO SEND UP TO FOUR MESSAGES
AT A TIME. BUT HE NEVER WAS ABLE TO CREATE
A BETTER TELEPHONE THAN THE ONE ALEXANDER
GRAHAM BELL INVENTED.

After their summer wedding in 1877, Mabel and Alec traveled to England for their honeymoon. It was supposed to be a romantic vacation, but Alec, as always, saw there was work to do. He wanted people in England to buy and use his telephone, too.

In London, Queen Victoria invited Alec to show her his telephone. Alec handed the queen the receiver. Right away, she heard people

speaking from three different cities in England. She thought Bell's telephone was "extraordinary." Alec was so happy, he reached out to touch the queen's hand. A gasp arose from the crowd. It was considered rude to touch the queen. But Alec had spent most of his life working with the deaf. For him, touching people was a natural way to communicate. The queen didn't seem to mind. She placed an order for a telephone. So did many other people. Soon Alec's telephones were installed in homes all over England.

Unfortunately, back in the United States, there was more trouble brewing. Western Union had started its own telephone company. It was called the American Speaking Telephone Company. Alec knew that this never should have happened. He owned the patent on the telephone.

To make matters worse, his own company was having trouble installing the wires needed for the telephones. Western Union could use telegraph wires for its telephones. The Bell Company had to start from scratch. The answer to the problem was telephone poles! However, it took time and money to put up the poles and string the wires. Bell Telephone was losing money fast.

What the company needed were more investors. New investors would put up money to keep the company going. Then later, when it started to make money (a profit), the investors would make money, too. Luckily, several Boston businessmen, including

WILLIAM H. FORBES

William H. Forbes, came to the rescue.

Now Bell Telephone had the money to compete with the American Speaking Telephone Company. The two companies battled for customers as more and more Americans wanted telephones. New jobs were created. People were hired to cut lumber for telephone poles. Workers were needed to string the wires on the poles. And telephone operators were hired to help people make their calls.

TELEPHONE OPERATORS

WHEN THE TELEPHONE FIRST CAME OUT, PEOPLE COULDN'T JUST DIAL A NUMBER THEMSELVES. FIRST THEY HAD TO SPEAK TO A TELEPHONE OPERATOR WHO PLACED THE CALL FOR THEM BY CONNECTING WIRES ON A SWITCHBOARD. THE FIRST TELEPHONE OPERATORS WERE TEENAGE BOYS. WHY? MANY YOUNG BOYS HAD WORKED IN TELEGRAPH OFFICES AND KNEW ABOUT SENDING MESSAGES. BUT A TELEPHONE

OPERATOR NEEDED PATIENCE. AND MANNERS. THESE WERE TRAITS THAT A LOT OF TEENAGE BOYS LACKED. SO, WOMEN WERE HIRED—WOMEN WHO HAD PLEASANT SPEAKING VOICES. EMMA MCNUTT WAS THE FIRST FEMALE OPERATOR. SOON, A CAREER AS A TELEPHONE OPERATOR BECAME THE SECOND MOST POPULAR JOB FOR WOMEN IN THE UNITED STATES. (BEING A TEACHER WAS THE MOST POPULAR.)

As for Western Union, the chief engineer, Elisha Gray, was once again accusing Alec of stealing the idea for the telephone from him. Mr. Hubbard decided the only way to stop Western Union from selling telephones was to go to court. Alec and Mabel were still in England and happy there. Mabel gave birth to a little girl on May 8, 1878. They called her Elsie May. But Western Union was too big a problem for Alec to remain

on the sidelines. It was urgent for Alec to come back to the United States to defend his telephone.

The court case dragged on for a year. In court, Alec and his partners presented their case. Alec had proof that he'd invented the telephone first. Although Western Union was a big, powerful company, as time went on they saw they were not going to win. On November 10, 1879, the case was settled. The Bell Telephone Company—and only the Bell Telephone Company—had the right to make and sell telephones.

Chapter 10
An Inventor to the End

Was that the last court fight over the telephone? Oh no. Many others tried to claim they'd invented the telephone. Over the years, Bell and his partners had to defend themselves in over six hundred cases! But they always won.

The Bell Telephone Company made Alec a rich man. However, Alec was growing tired of the telephone business. And, incredibly, he thought the telephone was a nuisance—he refused to have one in his own study! But worse, Alec's health was suffering. He had gained weight. He had trouble sleeping. His hair was going gray—and he was only thirty-two. Business problems were turning him into an old man. Alexander Graham Bell knew what he had to do. He was not

a businessman. He was an inventor! So, in 1880, Alec asked to leave the company. It was time to move on.

And move on he did. By this time, the Bells were living in Washington, DC. In his lab there, he developed a machine to give people hearing tests. It was called an audiometer. The machine sent out a series of different beeping tones—from loud to soft—to a device held against a person's ear. The units for sound volume were named bels. Alec never gave up on his mission to help the deaf and the hard of hearing.

THE DECIBEL OR THE BEL

LOUDNESS IS MEASURED IN DECIBELS. THE SYMBOL FOR DECIBELS IS DB. THE LOUDER THE SOUND, THE MORE DECIBELS. ON THE DECIBEL SCALE, THE LOWEST SOUND, WHICH IS ALMOST SILENCE, IS 0 DB. A SOUND THAT IS 10 TIMES MORE POWERFUL IS 10 DB. A SOUND THAT IS 100 TIMES MORE POWERFUL THAN SILENCE IS 20 DB. FOR EXAMPLE, A WHISPER IS 30 DB. A NORMAL CONVERSATION IS 60 DB. AND THE ROAR OF A JET ENGINE IS 140 DB.

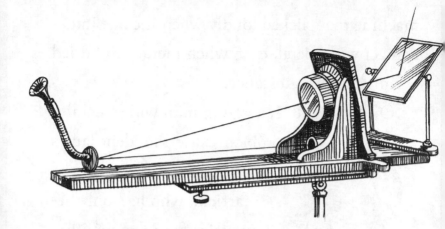

Not all of Alec's inventions caught on. Take, for example, the photophone. The idea behind it was to send sound on a beam of light. He was so proud of the photophone that he wanted to name his second daughter Photophone! Mabel would have none of that. They named the baby, who was born on February 15, 1880, Marian.

With another man, Alec also came up with a

machine that clicked loudly when it came into contact with metal, even when metal was buried within another substance.

On July 2, 1881, a young man with mental problems shot President James Garfield at a train station. Garfield, who had only been in office for a few months, did not die right away from the gunshot. But the bullet was lodged somewhere deep inside his body. The doctors thought that finding the bullet and removing it was the only chance Garfield had to recover. There were no X-ray machines at the time. So how could the doctors find the bullet?

PRESIDENT JAMES GARFIELD

Alec hoped that perhaps his metal detector

would show the doctors where the bullet was located. He visited President Garfield, who was in bed and in great pain. Alec passed the detector over his body. It reacted by making sound—too much sound to point out the exact location of the bullet. The experiment was a failure. President Garfield hung on for a couple of months, then died on September 19, 1881.

Bell was distraught. What had gone wrong? He had tested the machine many times. It had located a bullet that was lodged in a slab of meat.

It turned out that the problem wasn't Bell's machine. The problem was the president's bed.

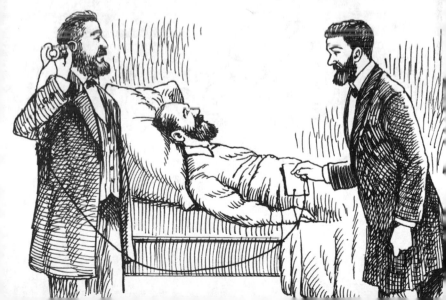

Metal-coil spring mattresses had just been invented. The president was lying on one of the very first ones. Bell's machine located all the metal coils as well as the bullet. Perhaps, if President Garfield had been lying on a feather bed, Bell's invention might have saved his life!

There was another life that Alec couldn't save. That of his own little baby boy. While Alec was trying to save the president, Mabel gave birth to their first son, Edward. It was August 15, 1881.

But the baby had come too early. He had trouble breathing. He did not live more than a few hours.

The Bells were heartbroken. For Alec, this great personal tragedy pushed him to invent a breathing machine. His hope was to save others. A metal jacket that he designed was wrapped around someone with breathing problems. A pump squeezed the jacket, and then stopped. It squeezed

again, then stopped. In this way, air was forced into and out of the person's lungs. Bell's metal jacket helped inventors develop the iron lung in 1928, a machine that saved many, many lives.

Alec couldn't stop working. Working was his life. But he was growing tired. He wasn't a young man anymore. He didn't have the same energy. The Bell family needed some time away. Baddeck, Nova Scotia, seemed like the perfect place to go. The Bells built a large house there, called Beinn Bhreagh (say: *Ben Vree-ah*). It means "Beautiful Mountain" in Gaelic. Winters were still spent in Washington, DC, but when the weather became too hot, the family retreated to the cool air of Nova Scotia.

Beinn Bhreagh didn't only offer cool weather and beautiful scenery; it offered plenty of room for the ever-curious Alec to do experiments. Since he was a child, Alec had been interested by flight. Could he create something that would enable

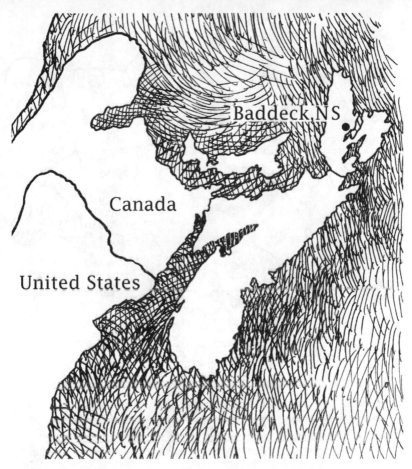

people to fly like birds? He started experimenting with kites. Kites would provide soft landings, he reasoned. After fifteen years he finally allowed someone to fly in one of his kites. However, it wasn't really flying. The kite just glided on wind

currents. It was the Wright brothers, Orville and
Wilbur, who invented the first airplane in 1903.
Still, Alec had fun creating kites in different
shapes—dogs, elephants, and more!

THE TETRAHEDRAL

ALEC TESTED MANY DIFFERENT SHAPES WHILE WORKING WITH KITES. ONE SHAPE, THE TETRAHEDRAL, PRODUCED THE FASTEST AND LIGHTEST KITES. THE SHAPE HAD FOUR TRIANGLES OF THE SAME SIZE (EQUILATERAL TRIANGLES) JOINED TOGETHER LIKE A PYRAMID. BELL ALSO REALIZED THAT THIS DESIGN COULD BE USED FOR BUILDINGS—NOT ONLY WAS IT LIGHT, BUT IT COULD SUPPORT A LOT OF WEIGHT. THE BUILDERS OF THE GEORGE WASHINGTON BRIDGE, WHICH CONNECTS NEW YORK AND NEW JERSEY, WERE AMONG THE FIRST TO USE ALEC'S IDEA IN THEIR CONSTRUCTION!

Alexander Graham Bell spent his life dedicated to science. In 1888, his father-in-law Gardiner Greene Hubbard helped start *National Geographic Magazine*. The magazine would cover many topics including nature, geography, foreign cultures, science, and technology. And after Mr. Hubbard's death, in 1897, Alec took over as president of the National Geographic Society, which published it. At that time, the magazine was small. Alec was determined to help it grow. He found a talented young editor named Gilbert H. Grosvenor to head the magazine. Together, the men helped the National Geographic Society become a very big and important organization. *National Geographic* is still published today, more than one hundred years later!

Grosvenor did more than help *National*

Geographic grow. He married Alec's daughter Elsie, and in time their son Melville Bell Grosvenor took over the National Geographic Society!

GILBERT H. GROSVENOR

Alexander Graham Bell was known to the world as an inventor. Yet he always saw himself as a teacher. He wrote, "recognition of my work for and interest in the education of the deaf has always been more pleasing to me than even recognition of my work with the telephone."

Giving someone deaf a way to break through their loneliness and communicate with other people—to Alec nothing was more important than that. In 1887, he agreed to meet with a deaf and blind girl named Helen Keller. Helen

had always behaved like a little wild animal. She threw tantrums all the time. Yet, upon meeting Alec, she calmly climbed up on his lap, and played with his pocket watch. Bell knew that although the little girl couldn't speak or hear or see, she could feel the vibrations of the ticking of his watch. Through Alec, the Kellers eventually found a teacher who was able to open the world to Helen. From that first meeting, Alec and Helen became lifelong friends, and Alec was very proud of Helen's accomplishments. Helen went on to college and became a world-famous speaker, political activist, and author.

Alexander Graham Bell was an inventor, a teacher, a husband, a father, and a friend. He would tell his students as well as his own children, "Don't keep forever on the public road, going only where others have gone, and following one after the other like a flock of sheep." Alec thought it was important to follow your own interests and see where they would take you. "Leave the beaten track occasionally and dive in the woods. Every time you do so you will be certain to find something that you have never seen before."

Alexander Graham Bell lived by these words. After he invented the telephone, he was rich. He didn't need to work for money. But he continued to work because of his curiosity. *Keep on fighting* were the words that hung on a sign in his lab.

KEEP ON FIGHTING

Alec lived by that motto. But age was slowing him down. He had gained even more weight. He suffered from a disease called diabetes.

On August 2, 1922, this great inventor died. He was seventy-five years old. Mabel was by his side. On the day he was buried, all telephone service was stopped in the United States for one minute. What a fitting way to honor  the man who not only invented the telephone, but devoted his life to helping people communicate with each other.

TIMELINE OF ALEXANDER GRAHAM BELL'S LIFE

1847	Born in Edinburgh, Scotland, on March 3
1857	Chooses the middle name Graham
1862	Moves to London to live with his grandfather
1863	Teaches at the Weston House Academy
1864	His father invents Visible Speech
1865	Grandfather Bell dies on April 23
1867	His brother Ted dies from tuberculosis
1870	His older brother, Melly, also dies from tuberculosis
1871	Teaches at the Boston School for the Deaf
1873	Begins teaching at Boston University
1876	Awarded the patent for the telephone on February 14
1877	Forms the Bell Telephone Company on July 9 Marries Mabel Hubbard on July 11
1878	His first daughter, Elsie May, is born
1880	Leaves the Bell Telephone Company His second daughter, Marian, is born
1881	Tries to help locate the bullet in fatally wounded President James Garfield
1887	Meets Helen Keller, who becomes a lifelong friend
1922	Dies on August 2

TIMELINE OF
THE WORLD

The tuning fork is invented by John Shore	1711
US Congress establishes the Library of Congress	1800
President Thomas Jefferson greatly expands the United States through the Louisiana Purchase	1803
Robert Fulton invents the first practical steamboat	1809
The War of 1812 ends	1814
Noah Webster publishes *An American Dictionary of the English Language*	1828
On May 24, Samuel F. B. Morse sends via telegraph the first electrically transmitted message	1844
Thomas Alva Edison is born on February 11	1847
Leon de Martinville invents the phonautograph	1857
The world's first underground railway opens in London Abraham Lincoln delivers the Gettysburg Address	1863
The United States turns one hundred	1876
Thomas A. Edison develops the first practical lightbulb	1879
President James Garfield is shot on July 2, 1881, and later dies from the bullet wound	1881
The Brooklyn Bridge, connecting Manhattan Island to Brooklyn, is completed	1883
The *Wall Street Journal* is first published	1889
Henry Ford drives his first completed automobile around Detroit	1896
The Wright brothers make the first powered plane flight at Kitty Hawk, NC	1903
The *Titanic* hits an iceberg on April 15 and sinks	1912

BIBLIOGRAPHY

*Berger, Melvin and Gilda. **Did You Invent the Phone Alone, Alexander Graham Bell?** Scholastic, Inc., New York, 2007.

*Carlson, Mary Kay. **Alexander Graham Bell: Giving Voice to the World.** Sterling, New York, 2007.

Crompton, Samuel Willard. **Alexander Graham Bell and the Telephone: The Invention That Changed Communication.** Chelsea House, New York, 2009.

*Fisher, Leonard Everett. **Alexander Graham Bell.** Atheneum, New York, 1999.

*Garmon, Anita. **Alexander Graham Bell Invents.** National Geographic, Washington, DC, 2007.

*Haven, Kendall. **Alexander Graham Bell: Inventor and Visionary.** Franklin Watts, New York, 2003.

*Matthews, Tom L. **Always Inventing: A Photobiography of Alexander Graham Bell.** National Geographic Society, Washington, DC, 1999.

*Pasachoff, Naomi. **Alexander Graham Bell: Making Connections.** Oxford University Press, New York, 1998.

*Venezia, Mike. **Alexander Graham Bell: Setting the Tone for Communication.** Children's Press, New York, 2009.

*Weaver, Robyn M. **The Importance of Alexander Graham Bell.** Lucent Books, San Diego, 2000.

* Books for young readers

YOUR HEADQUARTERS FOR HISTORY

Activities, Mad Libs, and sidesplitting jokes!
Discover the Who HQ books beyond the biographies